MINGLING WITH THE UNIVERSE

AN ULTIMATE GUIDE TO GET ANYTHING THAT YOU WANT BY CREATING YOUR LOVE STORY WITH THE UNIVERSE!

BANSI PATEL

Dedication

To my lovely Parents <3, my sweet brother Raj, my Mentor Amol sir and of course the Universe! Thank you for all the support and love!

TABLE OF CONTENTS

Chapter 1-Introduction

In April 2016, i.e. exactly, four months after I became a Chartered Accountant, I had a major meltdown. Becoming a Chartered Accountant was my dream and I had worked my buns off for achieving that dream. Now was the time to actually enjoy the fruits of all the hard work I had put in, so why wasn't I happy? I realized that I was not living I was just surviving. I didn't like my work and for hours in the office, I used to wonder about my life purpose, the meaning of life. But sadly, I was lost and couldn't find any future. All my friends were happy, travelling or getting married and I was STUCK in the same situation from like forever. There seemed to be no way out. It felt like I was trapped in a cage –A cage of fears, unhappiness, loneliness and discomfort. This fear soon took over me and I began to lose all my hope and positivity.

I started crying all the time- in washroom, on my desk, while driving and sometimes also during conversations with closed ones. There was no one place, where my fears did not follow me. I was clueless, helpless and hopeless. I was in that dark tunnel of uncertainty where there was no way to get out of it. It was clear darkness. I had not come *this far* to come just this far. This was a phase where I realized being successful does not mean being happy. I felt as if I was at the wrong place. I didn't have the courage firstly to accept that all this was not for me. Financially, my family had always struggled, and now was my time to earn and give my parents the happiness that they really deserved. They had struggled to fulfill every wish of mine, and it was now my turn to give them, a life more fulfilling. But the chaos inside me was driving me crazy. I was experiencing anxiety and insecurities 24*7. I had arguments with almost everyone around me. I felt as if People around me didn't want to understand me or my point of view. It was like I had two personalities, one which was giving fake smiles and showing to the world that I am Fine and the other the darker side, which only I knew. The side where I was lost and stuck and didn't find any way out in the complex maze called 'Life'.

One evening, I came back home from office, disgusted and thankfully no one was at home. I just kept my bag aside and cried like hell. I cried for almost two hours. I really needed someone to hug me, console me and assure me and say, "Don't cry beautiful, you are not alone. I am there with you always. You are a warrior, you can't break. Get up now and kill it". But I was too worked up to see any guidance around me. I finally opened a journal and wrote, "God, if you really exist, please help me. I feel alone. This anxiety will kill me. Please come down, I need you. Help me".

After this incidence, something miraculous started happening in my life. In this book, I will tell you my story about mingling with the Universe and show you exactly, what needs to be done, to connect with the Universe through workable simple steps. If you follow these steps I promise you will be able to connect and co-create anything that you want along with the Universe.

Many great teachers in the world like Oprah, Marianne Williamson, Rhonda Byrne, Wayne Dyer, etc. believe in this idea and have changed their lives and are changing lives around the world with their teachings.

Let's dive in with a smile. Each chapter will give you a new insight about co-creating anything you wish along with the Universe. Just keep an open mind and heart. Remember, wherever you are, in whatever situation you are, you can change your life and miracles will happen with your actions and willingness. Let's create your beautiful and one of a kind love story with the Universe!

Chapter 2. How it all started?

The next day after my breakdown, I reached office a bit early and was ready to welcome another shitty day ahead. But Universe had other plans. Now, the first thing I did before starting my work was to check mails. Not that it had some really fun stuff in my inbox, but it was a habit. But that day, along with the daily Horoscope, Dr. Batra, a few work mails and other promotional mails, I saw a mail from someone named Sam Brown. I didn't know who she was. I felt that mail landed into my inbox just out of the blue. After searching and googling a bit about her, I came to know that she was a blogger and a really awesome one. When I went through her mail, I was guided to Podcasts of Brooke Castillo. Hello, Podcasts? I had never heard of that before. Everything seemed alien to me. But god knows, why and how I actually downloaded the Podcast app and started listening to Brooke Castillo podcasts. It was as if, God was guiding me. But duh, why all this?

I felt it was just some coincidence and after listening to two or three podcasts which I really loved, I stopped listening to it. That day was pretty normal and thankfully I didn't have any argument with anyone and my mood was quite okay if not good.

I came back home and guess what, I received a notification of one Podcast added to the Brooke Castillo podcast series. I was intrigued. Why was I constantly being reminded of her? I as usual googled about her and came to know that she was a Life coach. When I read, "Life coach", I was confused. What on earth, does life coach mean? Anyways, I was least bothered, I continued to listen to her podcasts on "Study Yourself". Now, she taught a very simple and sorted model "Circumstances trigger thoughts cause feelings cause actions cause outcomes ". I know, it will be a bit difficult for you to digest, let me explain it to you in a simple way. This model was referred to as "Self coaching" model. It says that **"When you think a thought—you feel a feeling. When you feel a feeling—you take action, because of how you feel. Your actions (behaviors) create your experiences in the world and ultimately that is what your life looks like—your results".** I gradually began to study this model in detail and there I was. I finally started fixing the puzzled maze of life and understood exactly, why my circumstances are what they were. I constantly had sucking thoughts which created sucking feelings which led me to take sucking actions and ultimately sucking results.

I don't know why, but at that point, for the first time, I felt, I was being guided. Guided by whom? Universe, God, Spirit, whatever name you give. I used this model to become aware of my thoughts. Whenever any negative thought popped up into my head, I used to listen to music or podcasts or do anything to vanish that evil thought. After some days, it became a habit. I was naturally converting my negative thoughts into positive ones and it really worked. I gradually started doing better at my work.

This was the time of meeting my Love, the Universe for the first time. I still had no idea what was in store for me. This was just the beginning of my Love story with the Universe.

So, the first step in starting your love story with the Universe, is to ASK. Ask for its Love, its support. Believe me, from where I am right now in my life, it feels like "Universe is actually desperate to help you, it is you who has to just ASK! But just asking won't help.

"Sort Yourself".

Understanding why you are where you are is very important. Realizing that your life is what you have created so far is life-changing. By becoming aware that only you are responsible for your life, whether good or bad, makes it really easy to deal with rather than pondering "Why me always?" attitude . We become accountable for ourselves and responsible too.

Exercise-

Close your eyes and say "Dear Universe. I need your love right now. I know you are always there with me. Thank you! I know I am being Guided!" And think about this for seven to ten minutes (you can use a timer to keep a check on time). Whether you are happy or unhappy with your life right now? What is it that you want to change? Why do you want to change?

After doing it just take a book or a journal and write down your current scenario. Let the thoughts flow. Do not think and write, just free-write. All you have inside you will come up to the surface of your mind and will be reflected in your journal through writing.

Now, think about the thoughts you had regarding the current situation what you have just penned down.

Write down how you can replace those negative thoughts with positive thoughts. While doing this, Gratitude can really help. Think about the things you are grateful for, and write them down. There are ALWAYS things you can be grateful for, no matter how bad your current situation is.

After doing this first exercise, you will be able to clear up your mind which was earlier filled with clouds of doubts. You will understand yourself better and keep repeating to check your thoughts every day. Whenever any negative thoughts strike just punch it off with your sword of love and gratitude.

Through this step, you have taken the first step towards starting your love affair with the beautiful Universe. Congratulations!

Chapter 3. Busting off myths and decluttering the fears

I was constantly being guided by the Universe. Whenever, I was in certain situation or problem where I needed help, I was guided to the correct person, correct book, correct video or correct podcast which resolved my problem like a miracle. I had sensed that this miracle was nothing but the love I was receiving from the Universe. This was a very important phase where I had started developing my connection with the Universe. I had to keep my eyes open in order to see the guidance around me. While going through this process, I was able to declutter my false beliefs and mindsets. And oh boy, undoubtedly those mindsets and beliefs were BS and had not base at all.

Let us declutter some common myths, fears and mindsets in order to purify our minds, hearts and souls for welcoming the love from the Universe:

Myths:
1.All this ' Universe thing 'and thoughts cause things mentality is a thug- Well, those who think this way, are really blind to not see the love that is around them. Then they complain, why they are stuck in the same situations from forever. I am saying this because I also made the same mistake earlier and that is why I was having same unhappy life for over a decade! I know, if you are reading this Universe guidance thing for the first time, you will and you can doubt it. But just

because you do not believe it, does not mean it is not there. Millions of people have changed their lives by changing their thoughts and taking corrective actions. If this is not a miracle then what is?

2. It is too good to be true – As I said, I was being guided to correct books and people at the right time. Same is the incidence of my encounter with the book, "A Course in Miracles ". I was guided to read this book, when I had my fears always bothering me. "A Course in Miracles" refers to ego as fear. Fear will always try to dwell in when you are happy with your life or when something will be going on smoothly. For ages, I had been in fear. Fear of earning money for my family so that I can give them the life they deserve, fear of what if circumstances will not change, fear of not being good enough, fear of who am I to change anyone's life including my own, fear of being wrong, fear of high expectations and fear of dying every day. You see this fear had taken control of my life. I could not breathe. This was the main reason of my breaking down and crying for hours. Fear will always pop up when you will choose love. But trust me, love has hundred times more power than filthy fears. Don't let your fears crush your dreams.

3. Everything is planned- This is the most common myth. All that what is written in your life, is bound to happen, you cannot change it. Yes, so just be a puppet of your life, and watch the puppet show as the episodes are pre-written by Him. Like really? Wake up! Whatever is bound to happen will surely happen but that does not mean to become an audience of what's happening in your life. Millions of people have changed their lives from rags to riches, from no love to sea of love. How can anyone just blindfold himself and suffer in the name of "Everything is planned by Him"? This notion really contradicts whatever, this book is all about or whatever great teachers in the past have taught or are still teaching. You are responsible for your life and you can change your life. This is the truth. Period.

'A Course in Miracles' refers "miracle" as "A simple shift in perception". How true it is. I have been able to change my life by changing my perceptions about life. Miracles happen if you are willing to see them. Universe will never hold your hand or guide you if you are not willing to see it. This is a very vital step in creating a connection with the Universe. Busting all these myths and fears are necessary for taking a step forward in opening our hearts for the Universe to fill them with love.

Chapter 4- Just Ask for a drop of love and Youniverse will shower rains

The Love of Universe is really unconditional. It guides and loves you even when you feel unloved or unguided. I had just asked for help and opened my arms for support, but what I received was immense love and guidance much more than I had expected or asked.

I spent my free time reading books or watching videos of my virtual mentors. They really helped me declutter my fears and doubts. I had started understanding this whole process bit by bit. I felt as if Universe was always watching me secretly like a crush does and I had this big smile on my face when I felt the presence of this power around me. I started saying "Hey, that's you right! You did it. Thank you."

I had started living again. I no longer felt like a loser. I still hadn't found my life's purpose but I knew Universe was holding my hands now and was taking me towards it slowly but steadily. My fears began to reduce. I started feeling Free, for real. It was a magical feeling which I hadn't experienced before. Infatuation began to grow between me and Universe. *Blush blush.*

My heart trusted Universe. It knew, no matter what, I will be guided correctly and I will get to my unknown destination soon.

I started getting links of my now virtual mentors, from out of the blue. My Facebook page either had their links or I got a mail from somewhere. And books, oh god, I cannot tell you how magically I was being guided to read some books. Some one used to mention those out of nowhere or I would get books suggestions from my mentor through their videos and books. I was receiving guidance from the invisible.

Soon, I got a new task in office. Yes, it was about writing and publishing articles on income tax. Now, I know some of you might be scratching your heads by reading "Income tax", but it was my profession, folks. And guess what, I started enjoying it. I fell in love with writing and editing. I had butterflies in my stomach before clicking the "Publish" button. People started reading my articles and they were liking it. I was so happy. I started writing regularly. It not only improved my writing skills but also enhanced my tax knowledge. Now, I started feeling that I was doing the right thing.

I soon started my own blog (not on income tax but about Life in general) and got really good feedback on it. At that time, I don't know, how I missed to see, that Universe was guiding me to become a writer. Yes, I loved writing. Whenever free, I started writing on spirituality or productivity or success or anything that felt right at that moment. Many a times, I used to get my topics for blogs at midnight. Yes, actually! Universe was showering rains of love and guidance on me. I felt great and decided to keep writing.

Now, many of us, think we have to do this and that, get inspired by watching videos or reading books, but believe me, it's of no use, if you fail to take action. And there is no right time to start. You need not be perfect, you just need to start!

I trusted my intuition and guidance which I was receiving from the Universe and started taking baby steps. I still had no idea, where I was heading to, but I was sure, I was going to land somewhere, a beautiful unknown destination.

So, Next step for you is to accept love and guidance from the Universe with open arms and without doubting. Just go with the flow and see what future has in store for you!

Chapter 5- Love at NO sight!

The infatuation between me and Universe was slowly turning into Love! The guidance I was receiving was inexplicable and I was enjoying the attention I was getting. I mean, who doesn't enjoy attention? Well, I soon started providing excellent quality work in my workplace and my Boss and colleagues seemed to be really proud of me. I had started speaking up and taking initiatives. I had started loving myself again. It was as if I was reinventing myself in this whole process. My social life started getting better and many people wrote to me or started coming to me for assistance. I really loved helping them.

One day, I was reading a book called, "Girl Code" by Cara Alwill Leyba, and again, this book had pointed out the word "Life coach". This was not the first time where I was being introduced to the Life coach concept. I thought it is really not a coincidence and that I should research on it. Surprisingly, I was guided to mentors like Marie Forleo, Gabby Bernstein, Danielle LA Porte, etc. All these incredible women were making difference out there. They had shredded off their past beliefs and despite of so many challenges, had achieved great success. All these women inspired me like never before. It had become my routine to go to office, come back home and study –study about these amazing women, their work and great books. I had tapped into a whole new world, where everything seemed to be possible. It was like imaginationary second world. I started taking care of myself for the first time. I started meditating and eating healthy. I don't know how this invisible force was guiding me to do all the Right things I had never done before.

I was gaining that lost confidence in myself again. It was a phase of transformation for me. Every day I woke up with a zeal and enthusiasm of going out there and making a difference.

One day, there was a power failure in our office and thankfully my Laptop had good battery backup to keep going for about an hour or two. The moment there was a power failure, I had this google ad of an eminent Life Coach Training school, flashing on my Laptop. It was as if, that situation was purposely created by the Universe for me, to pay attention on that Google ad, as had there not been power failure, I would not have checked that google ad at all. I soon navigated the website of that school and don't know how but decided to enroll myself.

By that time, it was not that, our financial condition had changed or something, yes, situation was a bit better but still worse. Had it been the Old me, I would not have even thought of enrolling myself in the school owing to the financial crunch. But don't know how, this time, I was sure, I was doing the right thing.

I went home and discussed about it and told them about my decision and that I have already enrolled myself. And to my surprise, my parents were not angry. They just enquired about the training and were okay with it. My happiness knew no bounds, at that moment.

The other day, I told them, I will pay my first instalment for the life coach school from my salary and my parents agreed. After five days, was the due date of paying the fees and the moment I was going to make payment , I received a call from home, that they had to urgently pay the interest of loan we had taken, and if interest is not paid within time, our shop would be sealed. I obviously had to make the payment of bank interest first. Again, my dreams were going to crush in front of my eyes. Not paying the fees that day meant waiting for one whole year to start living my newly found purpose. My heart sank and I could not understand what Universe wanted from me. If it wanted me to enroll for the life coaching school why it did threw me into this situation now, where I had no option at all. But I decided to trust Universe. I was sure it will find a way out for me. At that point, one small part of my brain really thought I was being silly for trusting the unknown force so damn much but my heart, it was comparatively clear and knew something good will happen from this whole situation. And guess what, Universe did help me that day!

I was sitting sadly on my desk, when my Mentor cum Boss, came to me asked, "Hey, Are you fine? Everything, alright?"

I immediately answered, "Yes sir, everything okay!"

He gave me a perplexed look and said "Are you sure? You can tell me. Please tell me!"

Tears started bursting out of my eyes, I could hardly say anything. He offered me a glass of water and I explained my problem to him.

Within ten seconds, he said with a smile, "What! Such a small issue. I will do one thing, I will make the payment of your first instalment now, and you can start your training."

This was not the first time, he had appeared as an Angel in disguise, he had supported me always. So, I could not burden him more by asking help from him.

I denied taking any help and then he said, "Look, I am not doing something great okay. Come on girl, you can repay me later after becoming a life coach". He smiled. "And it is your dream, how can it be crushed?"

I felt better and made the payment of first instalment of my life coach school. I thanked him for a tons of times and I had not noticed before but he was always there to help me, whenever I needed a friend or a mentor. At that time, I realized, Universe really wanted me to become a Life Coach and that it had send My Mentor in my life for all the right reasons. I felt as if, Universe had always been there for my support, it was me who couldn't see it before. Sometimes, it sends some angels or spiritual guides to guide you. And my mentor was a one of the perfect examples of that.

I was so excited I was able to actually get into the Life coach school training. I soon started my training and loved it. I am now balancing a full time job along with Life Coach training and I am loving every bit of my life.

I now understand clearly, why everything had happened in the past and how it all was guiding me towards a better future. I was only evolving because of my circumstances. Had my circumstances not been this way, I would have never discovered my capabilities. A simple girl who always lived in her cocoon had evolved into a butterfly spreading joy and love wherever she went. All this was no coincidence. These were and are the showers of love from the Universe.

I am in Love with this invisible force, which loves me back with no expectations at all. It loved me before, it loves me right now and will always love me, no matter wherever I go. This love guides me to do right things and allows me to make mistakes and learn from those mistakes. This love that Universe gifts me every day never judges me for my choices or mistakes. It just wants me to be happy and to make others happy. It loves me when I don't even thank for his love or when I am too busy working. It loves me when I am a total mess or nagging. It just loves me. It was there from forever maybe, it was there in form of our Parents to be with me always. It cannot take care of us, always, so it sends Spiritual guides and angels to show us the right path. Its love is limitless. Its Love is the only Real thing in this world. I am in Love with the Holy Spirit, the Universe. I have not seen it, but felt it for sure. I was never touched it but embraced it for sure. I have fallen in Love with the Universe at NO sight at all. Our love is purest as we are connected with pure feelings and Love.

Chapter 6- Receiving love signals from Universe

In my relationship with the Universe, I don't know who proposed whom, but what I know for sure is that I have accepted the love that I am receiving with my mind, body and soul. There is no part of me, which is left unloved by the Universe. My soul has been purified by its love. You know what, when you start enjoying this process of transformation and gratefully accepting its love, miracles happen! Universe starts expressing its love in its own mystic ways. You will be surprised by its miraculous love signs.

Every day when I get back home from work, I have some *STILLNESS* time with myself. This is the time of surrendering yourself to the Universe. This is the time of letting go all your fears, egos and negative thoughts to be transformed into positive and magical ones. Just ten minutes of stillness each day, will magically connect you to the Universe. Why is it needed? Because it works. Period.

Each day, from the time we wake up, to get ready, to go to work, to come back, to go for outings, anything you do, is full of action and activity. You are running whole day, if not you, your mind is running behind thousands of thoughts. There has to be a pause for this chaos in your mind and body. Stillness provides the serenity and peace that is required to just calm down and relax. Stillness time is when you converse with the invisible force. It is the *Date* with the Universe. It is the time when you look inside yourself for all the peace required. I was even guided to this stillness by this invisible force. Yes, meditation. I tried it once and I loved it. I practice it every day for at least ten minutes. It really helps me declutter everything. Just everything that is going around me.

Over the last few months, I have deepened my connection with the Universe and it expresses its love in more expressive ways than Humans! Trust me. When I am done with meditating, I simply remove my journal and let my pen flow. And words I read after I finish scribing really fascinate me each day. I always feel a divine presence whenever I perform this exercise.

Every day, while driving to office, I see signs like "11, 22 33, 44, 55,999 ", all these are angel numbers. Each number combination has some meaning and it really brings a big smile on my face, when I see these signs everyday repeatedly. I have also experienced immediate responses, like when I say, "Thank you, Universe!" I immediately see a board on which "Welcome "is written. I also ask for signs when I need guidance and I always receive it. Sometimes, when I am unsure about whether I am right or wrong, I ask for guidance and I see, "God is with you" or "Well-done" or " You are right" signals on the cars or display boards or on a book . These signs are no coincidence, I can tell, because, coincidence happens once or twice not always. I am actually guided, whenever, I need it. Whenever, something is not good for me, that work or thing or client does not show up and later I realize that it was better it didn't turn out how I had planned. You see, when you surrender yourself to the Universe, it guides you to what it right for you not what you want!

When I look back at my problems in the past or some mean people in the past that I had encountered with, all were lessons. Universe wanted me to learn from those problems and people and evolve. Had those problems and people not planted into my life by the Universe, I had not been the person, I am today. Puzzle pieces are now falling into place. Now, I exactly understand how those people were placed in to my life and removed by the Universe when their role was over.

Try it! You too will surely receive signs from the Universe. The timing of these signs will depend on how deep your connection is with the Universe. For some, it may take time to develop that divine connect but once connected, that will remain intact if you are alert and have unwavering faith. You see it or not, you feel it or not, you are always being guided by the Universe. It is constantly sending you love signals, all you have to do is to just open your eyes to see it and open your heart to feel it. Universe works fast when you are having fun. So just have fun and play with it. It will surely astound you with its tricks and ways of expressing its love for you.

Till here, you are with me right?

Great! Now, I and Universe are officially in a relationship. Yes, a committed one. You too have to build a committed relationship with the Universe. Just be ready to love and receive love. It's that simple.

Chapter 7- Mingling with the Universe

I am on cloud nine. Usually, this is how everyone in love feels, right? Well, I am no different. I feel the same. Being in a committed relationship brings you love, care, comfort and happiness. I am living in this feeling of love every day now. I must say I am honest and loyal as well, like any true lover will be. I never doubt Universe for its decisions and have learnt to naturally surrender myself to it. But well, it doesn't mean I don't fight with it. I do have my own little cute fights with it but I realize that It is always Right. And like they say, "You want to be Right or Happy? " Well, I am happy being Happy!!

Like any relationship, this one, also demands you to be authentic! The more true you are to yourself, the more true you will be towards others and to the Universe. The Life Coach training is teaching me new ways to make difference in others life but more importantly it is teaching me how to coach myself first. I am growing day after day and exploring my relationship with the Universe through my Chartered Accountancy job, through the articles that I write, through my life coach training and through people I come across each and every day. These days, I focus on relaxing more opposite to what I was before who stressed on every small stuff. This is because I know, Universe has my back and that it will lead me where I am supposed to be. This trust is very important in any relationship or friendship.

Right now also, when I am writing this book, I can feel that divine presence around me. I feel as if someone is writing through me. Words are coming directly from my heart and it is what is bringing me happiness currently.

One important thing to remember in a good relationship is not taking your partner for granted. If you are surrendering yourself so much that you are not taking any action and let the Universe spoon feed you, then just stop there. Relationship works two ways okay. There is no one sided happy love story. You will end up getting yourself into trouble if you take Universe or its guidance and love for granted. Universe's work is to direct you, it is your work to take the action and get it done. Universe is the best and greatest Life coach. Like we learn in our training, "Coach will help you get whatever you want, but first you will have to tell him, what is it that you want and take actions as directed by the Coach".

Happiness will come only through equal love and trust of both in each other. Remember, mingling with anyone is a very divine, serious and responsible job. Do not wreck it up, if you are not ready for it. It takes total commitment for a relationship to grow and later to nurture the same. Make sure you are ready for it by busting all the myths and fears and by trusting the Universe that everything will happen for your highest good.

Being in a committed relationship with Universe helped my loneliness disappear. I am now happy and always busy doing something productive. I have started writing more often. This was a big change in me. I started being myself and being authentic in everything I did whether it was in my articles, in my job, in my training, with friends or relatives and even when alone.

Co-creating with the Universe requires your total commitment towards what you want to create as well as towards the Universe itself. It is a two sided affair. Your actions should reflect your sincerity towards what you want to achieve only then will the Universe support you and co-create with you.

When it comes to relationships or lifelong relationships, obviously staying in touch matters a lot! Same is with the relationship with the Universe. You have to stay connected and nurture your relationship with much love and passion every day. No matter how things get, never forget to establish your connection with it and you will be guided always.

Love multiplies by spreading it!

Love is a multiplying force. It will enhance when you spread it. Have you got something to gift to the world? Unique talents or knowledge? Then what are you waiting for *Just spread it.* Universe is made up of one essential nutrient called "Love" and you will receive it in abundance when you will share the same with others. So go ahead and spread love.

Remember that my job is to show you how to mingle with the Universe but you have to nurture your relationship with it. Each one has a unique experience about his or her relationship with the Universe. There is no standard or ideal form of relationship. Neither is any relationship perfect. After all, none of us are perfect. It is only the Universe who is perfect, right!

Chapter 8- Fear is the Villain in this love story

What happens when everything is going perfect in a relationship? Guess! Yes, the Villain creeps in. Fear or ego as "A course in Miracles" refer to, is the main villain in your love story with the Universe. It will dwell in the moment you feel your life is dreamy or it is too good to be true. It is not your fault. Since childhood, we are being programmed that Life is supposed to be a struggle and that without any sorrows or problems life is impossible but that does not mean, life cannot be fantastic or the way you want. Of course, it can be! Many people out there are living the life of their dreams.

In this chapter, I will show you how to kick off your fears and stay connected with your love, Universe.

A Course in Miracles says, "The ego seeks to divide and separate. Universe or Spirit seeks to unify and heal." Where does this ego come from? Well it comes from Judgment! *How can my life be so smooth, why is he loving me so much, I am not good enough, Do I deserve so much love, No, all this cannot be true, it is just a temporary phase, it will pass and I will again fall back to where I had started from.* All these are Judgments come when you allow your fears or egos to take control of your thoughts.

Remember, Circumstances trigger Thoughts cause Feelings cause Actions cause Results.

One negative situation you land in and then you are tempted to make judgments and attract negative thoughts which in turn will cause you to take wrong actions and get all the wrong outcomes. So beware, one thought and judgment can really let ego win.

Now, you will ask, it is possible to stay aware of our thought patterns and to live so consciously that no negative thoughts trigger at all?

Of course, it's not. If you will be so conscious then probably you will be living in fear 24*7, it by default means you are not living at all. So, how to deal with it?

Practice. Yes, simply practice every day. Don't try to control your emotions or feelings otherwise it will burst out some day like an overblown balloon. Just do not make Judgment. Feeling angry? Fine. Feel it. Calm yourself down. Understand what made you angry. Becoming aware of these thoughts alone, can change your whole system of thinking. At the time of your Stillness, understand that whole situation and try to clear your thoughts about it. Deepen your connection with the Universe more and more when you feel like you are getting infected with negative thought patterns. Remember, Fear wants to separate YOUNIVERSE into you and Universe, do not let that happen. Till today, I am fighting with my fears and ego but the best part is now instead of them taking control over me, I am controlling my ego. This way, I am able to strengthen my bond with the Universe.

Love is the most powerful force in the world. No big villain can survive against it. The size of your fears is only how much you give importance to it. Love is million times more powerful than fear. Do not let your pea sized fear ruin your relationship with Universe. Trust the Universe. Its love is unconditional.

Last but not the least, practice TO FORGIVE. Forgive yourself for making judgments. Forgive the person who made you angry. Just forgive. It will bring the peace. A Course in Miracles says "Do you want a quietness that cannot be disturbed, a gentleness that never can be hurt, a deep abiding comfort, and a rest so perfect it can never be upset? All this forgiveness offers you, and more"

Forgiveness is the greatest gift you can give yourself. By forgiving the one who had inflicted you wounds, you will not only heal your pain internally, but one day, the marks of such wound will also disappear. By forgiving, you are choosing peace of mind for yourself. You cannot be happy from within unless your heart is burden less, it has no grudges against anyone. You cannot move on, unless you forgive and forget your past who has shaken you so deeply. Forgiveness will not change your past, but it will surely shine your future.

Chapter 9- Trusting the Youniverse and surrendering yourself

Fears and ego are not one time villain, who will disappear permanently. It is that "You Know Who" who used to always come back in Harry Potter's life in some or the other form. They will disappear for some time and again start popping in when you are in a negative mood like angry, sad, jealous, insecure or guilty. Remember, the only way to fight the battle with these fears is by being one with the Universe.

It is impossible to battle against Youniverse and your fears will have to give up. But first, you will have to surrender yourself totally to the Universe. Have trust in it, especially, when things seem to be out of your control. Universe will take care of it. It will also guide you to the people and resources required to shed off your fears.

I will share my story about how Universe helped me get out of a big trouble.

At that time, I was lonely and I really wanted someone to care of me and to love me. My friends were in relationships and some were even getting married. All this led me to create thoughts of having a partner. As you know, thoughts become things. A very handsome guy came in my life out of the blue, but little did I know, about his plans.

He proposed me the day he met me and I don't know why, but I wasn't ready. I felt as if Universe is giving me signs that he is not the one for me. After I met him, my daily plans got disturbed. I couldn't give enough time to write or even study my course material. This really frustrated me. Afterwards, I understood that I was wasting my time with a loser who was only interested in money and material pleasures and was going to become a big hurdle between me and my dreams. I decided to tell him not to ever meet me again. But he was filthy and sticky as Fears. He started stalking and irritating me. One fine evening I decided to just confront him and tell him once and for all to stay away from me. We decided to meet at a local restaurant. To my surprise, he came with his friends and he started humiliating me for ignoring and rejecting him. Soon, my angel in disguise was sent. One of my clients was in the same restaurant that evening. By that time, the client had sensed there was some issue. Soon within five to ten minutes he came in along with the Security guards like a hero. I knew, Universe had sent him. That day, I learnt a big lesson. Looks do not matter. Someone can be good looking but a total loser as that guy was. Lesson number two I learnt was, always ask for your partner for getting into a relationship when you are ready for it. My Career was my boyfriend and I wasn't ready for any relationship. But as they say, you learn from your mistakes.

It was my trust in Universe and being aware of my thoughts that really saved me. Universe will give you whatever you want, even if it is bad choice. Universe is a spoiler too. It will spoil you with its love. So be very careful when you ask anything from it.

Establish a divine and spiritual relationship of your own understanding. It will surely grow, but first you will have to learn to honor your own relationship with the Universe.

Chapter 10- Who Wins the Love battle?

By far I have told you how I started my relationship with the Universe, how I deepened my connection with it and how I fought my ego and fears by busting those false beliefs by choosing the path of LOVE.

All this transformation has happened within less than twelve months. That is like really quick, right? It will happen with you as well if there is a willingness to change and your unwavering trust on the Holy Spirit or Universe.

I have gone through and am still going through this process of transformation. Trust me, it is like magic.

There was a time I felt I can never get out of this trap that was created by my fears, anxiety and insecurities. But look at me, now. I Am a Changed women. This change is not less than any Miracle. Every bit of a change in my personality, in my beliefs, in my thought patterns and in my life is brought by that Ultimate force –Universe or God. I feel fulfilled now. I have found my life's purpose. It is to teach about the force and the power that each one has within himself. Through my articles and blogs, through my assignments with my clients and also in my life coach training I reflect whatever I have learnt till now.

I have seen miracles happen myself. This feeling of security, this comfort, this assurance that I am being taken care of, is priceless. I have seen several people around me, who are only Surviving. They are not living at all. Some are running behind money, some are running behind fame and some behind one another.

I am trying to bust these false mindsets that achieving some particular thing or goal or rather a particular person will give them happiness. Happiness is within you, why are we searching it outside?

The whole Universe or spirit or soul that is within you is the only ultimate source of happiness. The sooner you realize it, the better your life will be.

Regarding the battle between my fears and my love for Universe? Is there even any need to tell you who wins always?

Temporarily, sometimes, my fears win but only for a short period of time. It is natural. But I am able to soon choose love instead of fear and it is like Universe hugs me daily for choosing love always.

To Dear Universe,

Every Love story is Unique But ours is my favorite.

Thank you for being with me always and for co-creating abundance.

Abundance of love, abundance of joy, abundance of knowledge, abundance of faith and for brightening up every area of my life. I am sure, we will work this way forever and continue to co-create and spread love.

Thank you for gifting me incredible people in my life.

Thank you for being there, when I was lost and alone.

Thank you for being there with me forever, till my last breathe. Love always wins!

Chapter 11- Living happily ever after.........

Like in a marriage, two souls unify to become one in order to spend a whole life together, same is with Youniverse. You have to become one. Oneness will set you free. Free from all the fears, sin feelings, guilt, hatred, jealousy, insecurities, etc. It will align you with Love. I know it is not possible to be happy always or to smile always. But a simple shift in my perception has opened doors of happiness for me. It has speeded up my career. I am inspiring others to live a life of their dreams. I have an awesome family and I feel more confident and one with the Universe.

Look, everyone will have different degrees of difficulties in life. Everyone will come from a totally different background and everyone's life experiences are also different. But what is common amongst us all is the ability to understand our thought patterns and loving from our hearts.

Your Youniverse love story can be totally different from mine or more dramatic than mine. But creating this connection is most essential. Once created, this connection goes on deepening and you will see some miraculous shifts in your life, like I did.

Remember one thing, there is always something you will have to be grateful for no matter how worst your life is currently. You have eyes through which you are reading, you have workable body, and you have family. There is always something to be grateful for. Whenever, you feel you are not in alignment with the Universe, just write down all the things you are grateful for and you will instantly start feeling good. It will not only make you feel good but unconsciously change your negative thought patterns into positive ones.

Everyday just wake up and embrace the love that Universe has to offer you. Be passionate about whatever you do. Bring that Fire on! Your collective efforts along with Universe's guidance will help you co-create JUST ANYTHING you want! Why to do it? Because it works like magic!

This was my love story with the Universe. Very soon, we will complete our one year of togetherness. Journey till now with Universe was miraculous. I am excited to know how many more surprises does future has in store for me!

Great luck to you all for starting your love stories with the Universe.

Spread love, Be Grateful, Expect Miracles and Choose Love always- Recipe for living happily every day.

ABOUT THE AUTHOR

Bansi Patel is a Chartered Accountant, blogger and a Life Coach by Profession. She lives in Nasik, India. Bansi loves educating and inspiring people to succeed and live the life of their dreams. She is a Light worker and it's her passion to spread light in the world through her work.

ONE LAST THING

If you enjoyed this book or found it useful I'd be very grateful if you'd post a short review on Amazon. Your support really does make a difference and I read all the reviews personally so I can get your feedback and make this book even better.

Thanks again for your support!

Printed in Poland
by Amazon Fulfillment
Poland Sp. z o.o., Wrocław